T0414258

Arcoíris

Grace Hansen

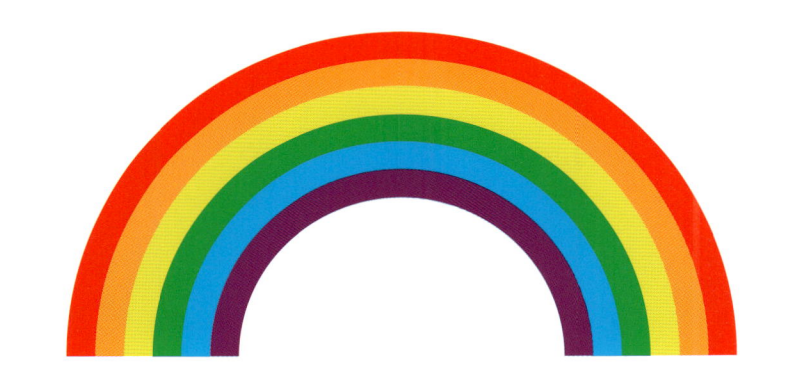

Abdo Kids Jumbo es una subdivisión de Abdo Kids
abdobooks.com

abdobooks.com

Published by Abdo Kids, a division of ABDO, P.O. Box 398166, Minneapolis, Minnesota 55439. Copyright © 2022 by Abdo Consulting Group, Inc. International copyrights reserved in all countries. No part of this book may be reproduced in any form without written permission from the publisher. Abdo Kids Jumbo™ is a trademark and logo of Abdo Kids.

Printed in the United States of America, North Mankato, Minnesota.

052021

092021

THIS BOOK CONTAINS RECYCLED MATERIALS

Spanish Translator: Maria Puchol

Photo Credits: Alamy, iStock, Science Source, Shutterstock

Production Contributors: Teddy Borth, Jennie Forsberg, Grace Hansen
Design Contributors: Dorothy Toth, Pakou Moua

Library of Congress Control Number: 2020930692

Publisher's Cataloging-in-Publication Data

Names: Hansen, Grace, author.

Title: Arcoíris/ by Grace Hansen;

Other title: Rainbows. Spanish

Description: Minneapolis, Minnesota: Abdo Kids, 2022. | Series: Luces en el firmamento | Includes online resources and index.

Identifiers: ISBN 9781098204495 (lib.bdg.) | ISBN 9781098205478 (ebook)

Subjects: LCSH: Rainbows--Juvenile literature. | Colors--Juvenile literature. | Prisms--Juvenile literature. | Light--Juvenile literature. | Astronomy--Juvenile literature. | Spanish language materials--Juvenile literature.

Classification: DDC 535.6--dc23

Contenido

Ilusiones en el cielo 4

Luz y energía 6

¿Cómo ver un arcoíris? 12

Más datos 22

Glosario 23

Índice 24

Código Abdo Kids 24

Ilusiones en el cielo

¿Has visto alguna vez un arcoíris? ¿Sabías que no es real? ¡Los arcoíris son **ilusiones** en el cielo!

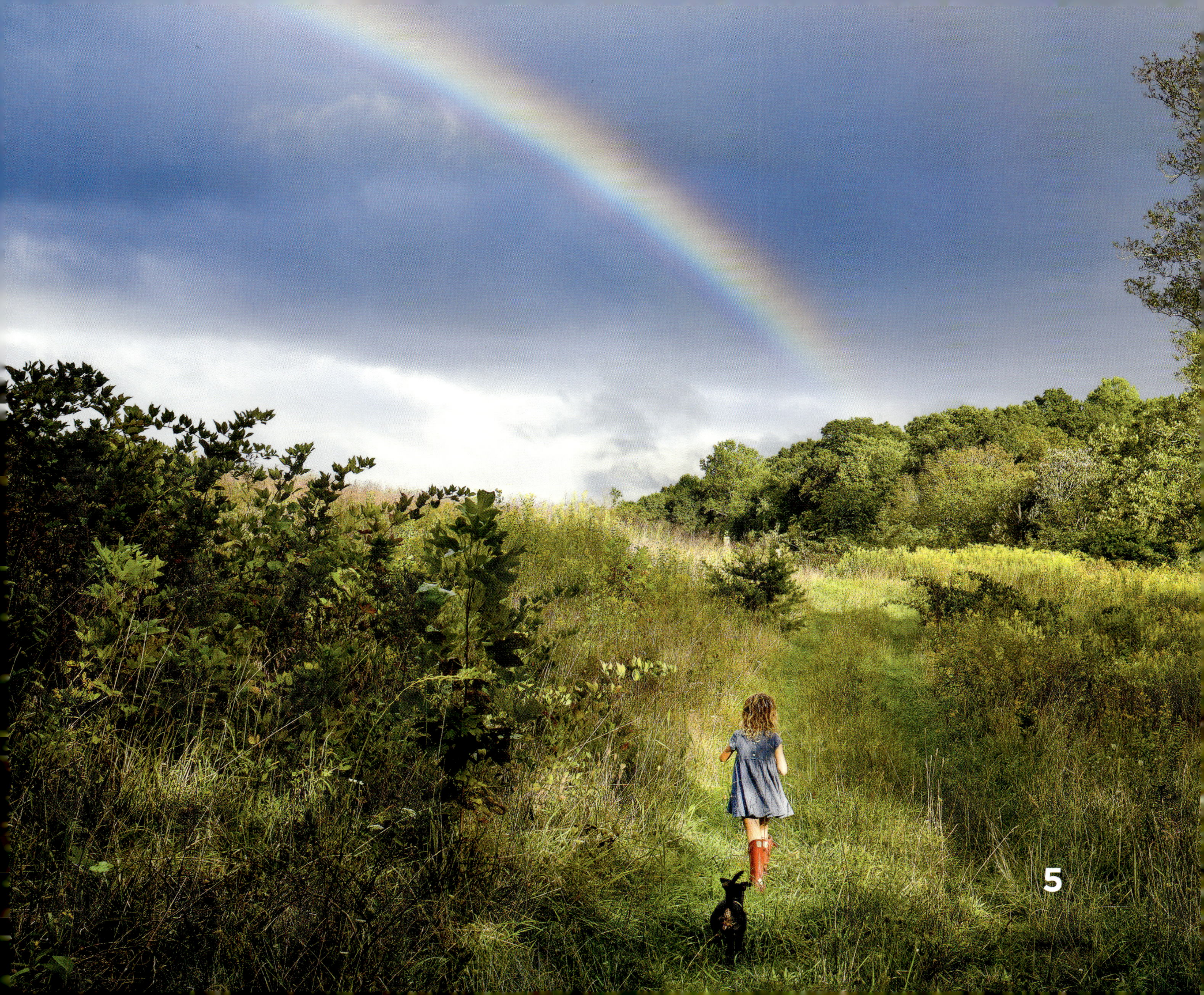

Luz y energía

La luz es una onda. La luz también es energía. La energía de la luz está conectada a su **longitud de onda**.

7

El rojo tiene una **longitud de onda** más larga. Esto significa que tiene poca energía. El violeta tiene una longitud de onda más corta. Esto significa que es alto en energía.

ROJO
longitud de onda:
~680nm

NARANJA
longitud de onda:
~610nm

AMARILLO
longitud
de onda:
~580nm

CIAN
longitud
de onda:
~490nm

VERDE
longitud
de onda:
~530nm

VIOLETA
longitud
de onda:
~410nm

Las ondas luminosas del Sol son las únicas que las personas ven. La vista identifica ondas como colores. Todos estos colores juntos se llaman luz blanca.

11

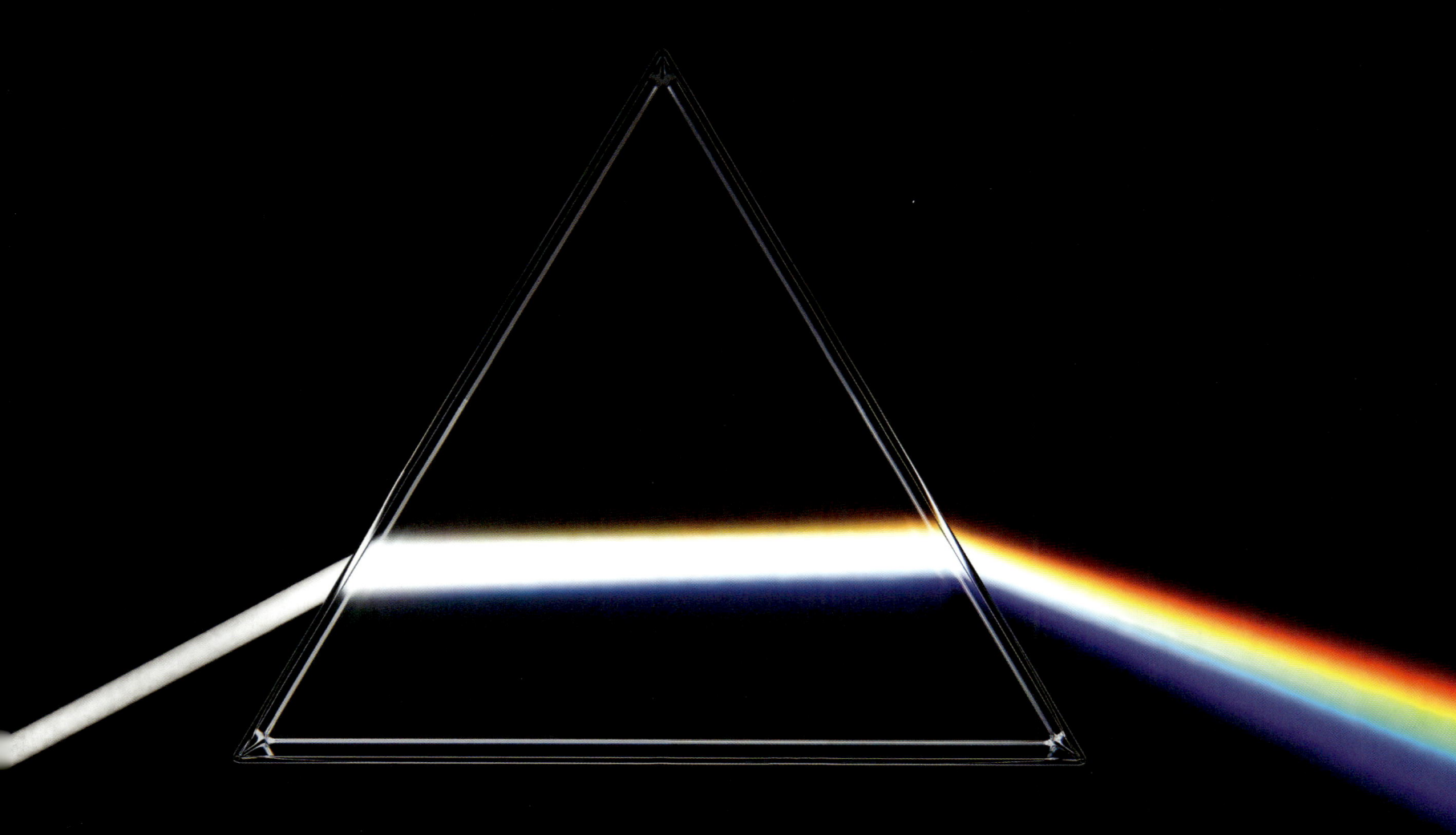

¿Cómo ver un arcoíris?

A menudo vemos arcoíris en la mañana temprano o a última hora de la tarde. Es porque el Sol está más bajo en el cielo.

13

Para ver el arcoíris el cielo debería estar lluvioso o **neblinoso**, y la luz del sol tiene que venir de detrás.

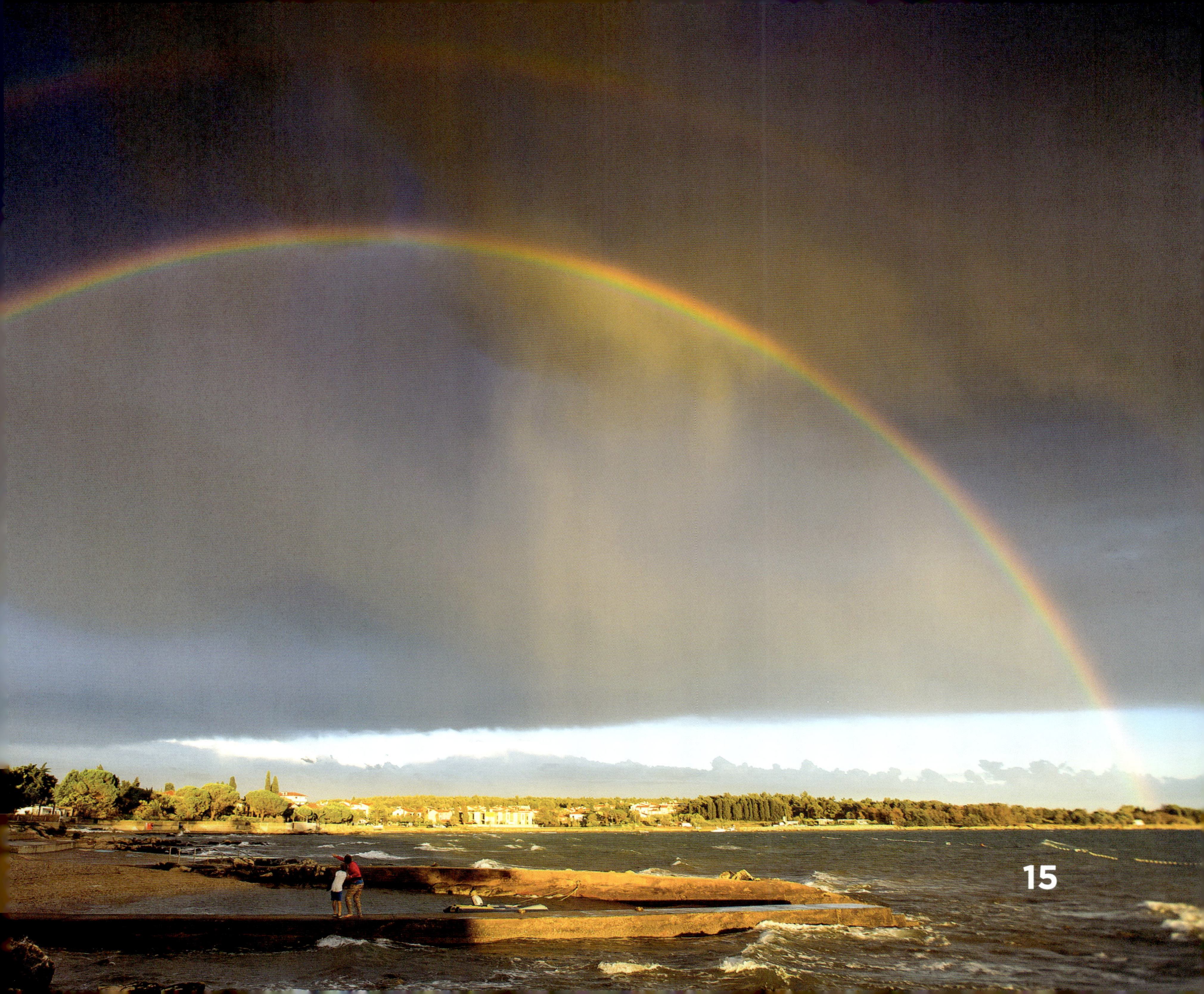

La luz del sol alcanza las gotitas de agua y esto hace que la luz se divida. Las diferentes **longitudes de onda** de la luz forman **ángulos** diferentes. Lo que causa que la luz blanca se separe.

luz solar

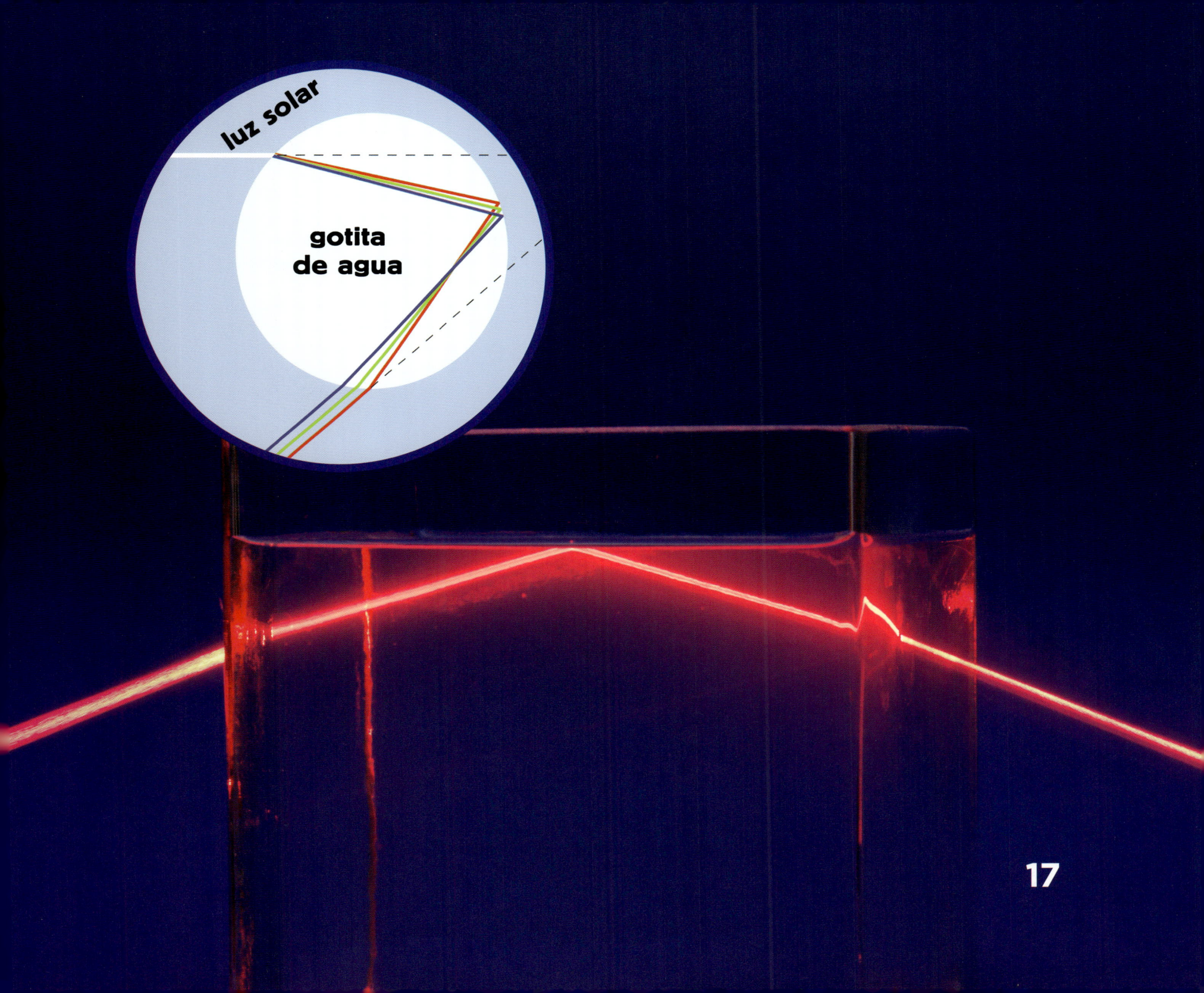

gotita
de agua

17

Entonces la parte posterior de la gota refleja la luz. La luz sale de la gota de lluvia en **ángulo** hacia quien la observa. El arcoíris se ve cuando sale de la gota.

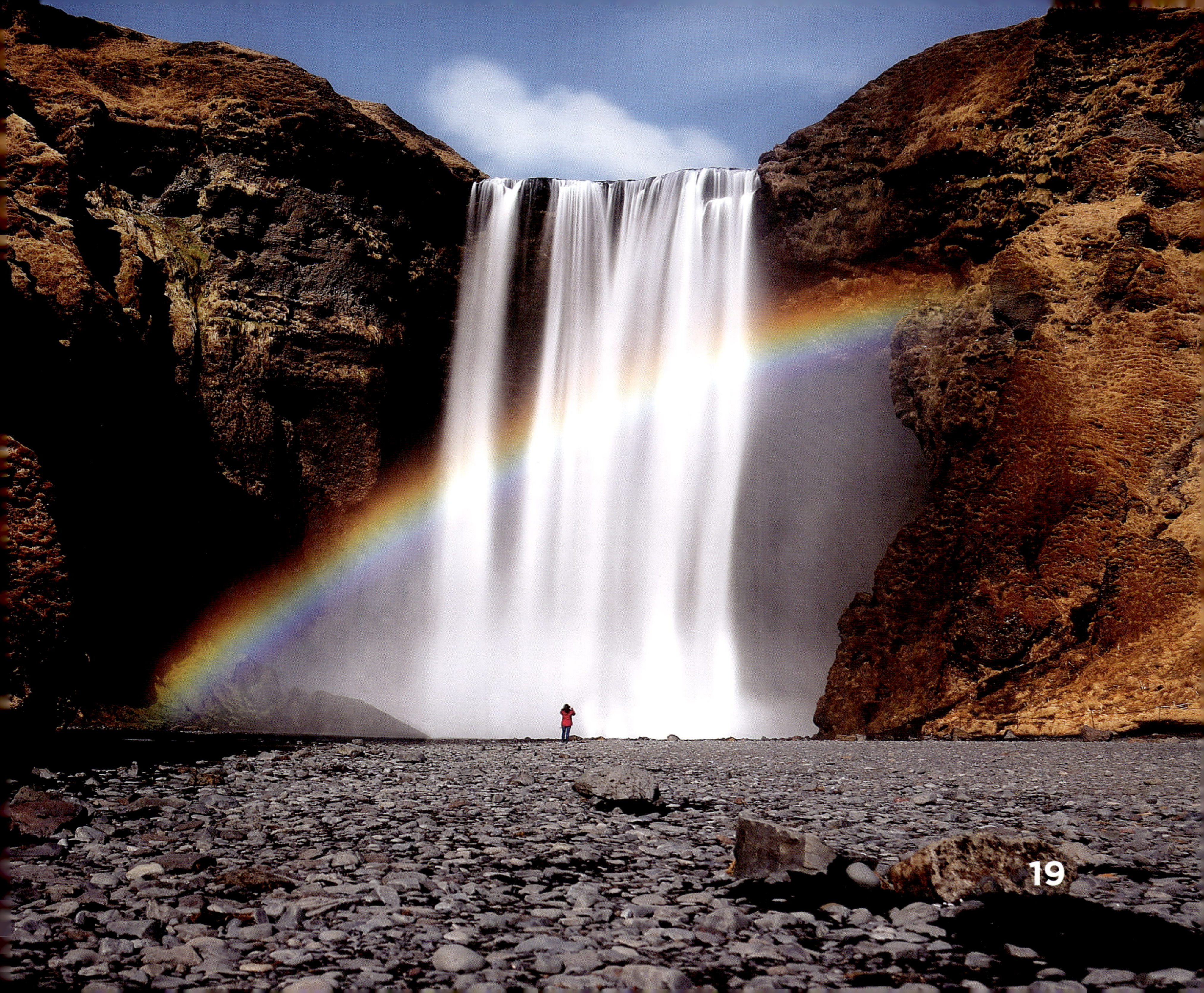

La luz roja sale en un **ángulo** de 42 grados. El ángulo del violeta es de 40 grados. Todos los demás colores están entre esos dos. Por eso los colores del arcoíris siempre están en el mismo orden.

21

Más datos

- Los colores del arcoíris son 7, rojo, naranja, amarillo, verde, azul, índigo y violeta.

- Incluso dos personas, una al lado de la otra, observan dos arcoíris diferentes. Porque están mirando las gotitas desde un **ángulo** ligeramente diferente.

- Cuanto más bajo esté el Sol, más alto estará el arcoíris en el cielo.

Glosario

ángulo - figura formada por dos líneas rectas que se cortan en un punto.

ilusión - representación no real, vista por el engaño de los sentidos.

longitud de onda - distancia entre dos picos de una onda.

neblinoso - lleno de llovizna. La llovizna es una nube de pequeñas gotitas de agua en la atmósfera.

Índice

agua 14, 16, 18

color 8, 10, 16, 20

energía 6, 8

longitud de onda 6, 8, 16

luz 6, 8, 10, 16, 18, 20

Sol, el 10, 12, 14, 16

ver 12, 14, 16, 18

Abdo Kids ONLINE
FREE! ONLINE MULTIMEDIA RESOURCES

¡Visita nuestra página **abdokids.com** para tener acceso a juegos, manualidades, videos y mucho más!

Los recursos de internet están en inglés.

Usa este código Abdo Kids
SRK9104
¡o escanea este código QR!

TIME FOR KIDS
BOOK OF WHAT

EVERYTHING ANIMALS

TIME FOR KIDS

Managing Editor, TIME For Kids: Nellie Gonzalez Cutler
Editor, Time Learning Ventures: Jonathan Rosenbloom

Book Packager: R studio T, New York City
Art Direction/Design: Raúl Rodriguez and Rebecca Tachna
Writer: Catherine Nichols
Illustrator: Chris Reed
Photo Researchers: Miriam Budnick, Elizabeth Vezzulla
Designers: Fabian Contreras, Ames Montgomery
Copyeditor: Joe Bomba
Indexer: Charles Karchmer
Fact Checkers: Luis Pereyra, Audrey Whitley

Redesign: Downtown Bookworks, Inc.
Project Manager: Sara DiSalvo

Cover: Symbology Creative

TIME INC. BOOKS

Publisher: Margot Schupf
Vice President, Finance: Vandana Patel
Executive Director, Marketing Services: Carol Pittard
Executive Director, Business Development: Suzanne Albert
Executive Director, Marketing: Susan Hettleman
Publishing Director: Megan Pearlman
Associate Director of Publicity: Courtney Greenhalgh
Assistant General Counsel: Simone Procas
Assistant Director, Special Sales: Ilene Schreider
Assistant Director, Finance: Christine Font
Senior Manager, Sales Marketing: Danielle Costa
Senior Manager, Children's Category Marketing: Amanda Lipnick
Associate Production Manager: Amy Mangus
Associate Prepress Manager: Alex Voznesenskiy
Associate Project Manager: Stephanie Braga

Editorial Director: Stephen Koepp
Art Director: Gary Stewart
Senior Editors: Roe D'Angelo, Alyssa Smith
Managing Editor: Matt DeMazza
Editor, Children's Books: Jonathan White
Copy Chief: Rina Bander
Design Manager: Anne-Michelle Gallero
Assistant Managing Editor: Gina Scauzillo
Editorial Assistant: Courtney Mifsud

Special thanks: Allyson Angle, Keith Aurelio, Katherine Barnet, Brad Beatson, Jeremy Biloon, John Champlin, Ian Chin, Susan Chodakiewicz, Rose Cirrincione, Assu Etsubneh, Mariana Evans, Alison Foster, Kristina Jutzi, David Kahn, Jean Kennedy, Hillary Leary, Samantha Long, Kimberly Marshall, Robert Martells, Nina Mistry, Melissa Presti, Danielle Prielipp, Babette Ross, Dave Rozzelle, Matthew Ryan, Ricardo Santiago, Divyam Shrivastava

Copyright © 2012 TIME FOR KIDS Big Book of WHAT

Copyright © 2015 Time Inc. Books. All TIME FOR KIDS material © 2015 by Time Inc. TIME FOR KIDS and the red border design are registered trademarks of Time Inc.

Contents of this book previously appeared in TIME FOR KIDS Big Book of WHAT.

For information on TIME FOR KIDS magazine for the classroom or home, go to TIMEFORKIDS.COM or call 800-777-8600. For subscriptions to SI KIDS, go to SIKIDS.COM or call 800-889-6007.

Published by TIME FOR KIDS Books,
An imprint of Time Inc. Books.
1271 Avenue of the Americas, 6th floor
New York, NY 10020

All rights reserved. No part of this book may be reproduced in any form or by any electronic or mechanical means, including information storage and retrieval systems, without permission in writing from the publisher, except by a reviewer, who may quote brief passages in a review.

ISBN 10: 1-61893-389-2
ISBN 13: 978-1-61893-389-8

TIME FOR KIDS is a trademark of Time Inc.

We welcome your comments and suggestions about TIME FOR KIDS Books. Please write to us at: TIME FOR KIDS Books, Attention: Book Editors, P.O. Box 361095, Des Moines, IA 50336-1095
If you would like to order any of our hardcover Collector's Edition books, please call us at 800-327-6388 (Monday through Friday, 7 a.m.–9 p.m. Central Time).

1 QGT 15

PHOTO CREDITS

Cover: Mark Wainwright/Symbology Creative (bkgrnd); Andreas Meyer/Shutterstock.com (narwhal); Suchatbky/Shutterstock.com (horseshoe crab); aabeele/Shutterstock.com (nautilus); Galyna Andrushko/Shutterstock.com (trees); ©iStockPhoto/GlobalP (sifaka); Michal Ninger/Shutterstock.com (kookaburra); C.K.Ma/Shutterstock.com (water); Baishev/Shutterstock.com (jellyfish); Mila Atkovska/Shutterstock.com (dog). Interior: 1: Mark Wainwright/Symbology Creative (bkgrnd); John Carnemolla/Shutterstock.com. 2–3: Shutterstock.com/watchara. 3: Richard Peterson/Shutterstock.com (elephant); Piotr Marcinski/Shutterstock.com (hand); oksana2010/Shutterstock.com (basketball). 4–5: Aleksandr Bryliaev/Shutterstock.com (bkgrd); Andrew Kerr/Shutterstock.com (dog). 5: Erik Lam/Shutterstock.com. 6–7: Aleksandr Bryliaev/Shutterstock.com. 6: reptiles4all/Shutterstock.com. 7: hammett79/Shutterstock.com (zebra); Rita Kochmarjova/Shutterstock.com (horse); Four Oaks/Shutterstock.com (elephant); Stuart G Porter/Shutterstock.com (lion). 8–9: Jennifer Gottschalk/Shutterstock.com (bkgrd); javarman/Shutterstock.com (aye-aye). 9: Naeblys/Shutterstock.com (globe); Joe McDonald/Shutterstock.com (sifaka). 10: Four Oaks/Shutterstock.com (elephant); Matt Gibson/Shutterstock.com (trunk). 11: Shutterstock.com (bkgrd); Richard Peterson/Shutterstock.com (elephant); Byelikova Oksana/Shutterstock.com (trunk). 12: Shutterstock.com (bkgrd); Michal Ninger/Shutterstock.com (kookaburra). 13: Evikka/Shutterstock.com (bkgrd); kzww/Shutterstock.com (herring). 14–15: schankz/Shutterstock.com. 14: chungking/Shutterstock.com. 15: sunsetman/Shutterstock.com (mudskipper top); Ivan Kuzmin/Shutterstock.com (mudskipper bottom); Erni/Shutterstock.com (axolotl). 16–17: Vladislav Gajic/Shutterstock.com (bkgrd); dkvektor/Shutterstock.com (illo); NOAA/OAR/OER/Dr. Kristin Laidre (narwhals). 17: National Institute of Standards and Technology/Glenn Williams. 18–19: Peter Zijlstra/Shutterstock.com (bkgrd); Map Resources/Shutterstock.com (globe); worldswildlifewonders/Shutterstock.com (platypus); ©iStockPhoto/IainStych (puggle). 18: John Carnemolla/Shutterstock.com. 19: Morphart Creation/Shutterstock.com. 20–21: Henrik Larsson/Shutterstock.com. 21: Stuart Ramson/Nothing But Nets (family); almondd/Shutterstock.com (jellyfish); Oksana Potyomkina/Shutterstock.com (hippo); Guy J. Sagi/Shutterstock.com (deer). 22–23: schankz/Shutterstock.com (bkgrd); Marques/Shutterstock.com (horseshoe crab). 22: OlegD/Shutterstock.com (living); MarcelClemens/Shutterstock.com (fossil). 23: antpkr/Shutterstock.com (cockroach); Vudhikrai/Shutterstock.com (chambered nautilus); AlessandroZocc/Shutterstock.com (coelacanth). 24–25: Andrii Muzyka/Shutterstock.com. 24: Image courtesy of the National Institute on Aging/National Institutes of Health. 25: Image courtesy of the National Institutes of Health. 26–27: Serg64/Shutterstock.com. 26: Be Good/Shutterstock.com (books); Shutterstock.com (numbers); agsandrew/Shutterstock.com (music); siamionau pavel/Shutterstock.com (painting). 27: Jaimie Duplass/Shutterstock.com (girl); Maksim Shmeljov/Shutterstock.com (hands); djgis/Shutterstock.com (flowers). 28–29: Puzyrna Galyna/Shutterstock.com (bkgrd); Blend Images/Shutterstock.com (girl). 29: s_bukley/Shutterstock.com (Thorne); Featureflash/Shutterstock.com (Knightly, Spielberg); Helga Esteb/Shutterstock.com (Cruise). 30–31: Sergieiev/Shutterstock.com. 30: Vladimir Wrangel/Shutterstock.com. 31: Creations/Shutterstock.com (heart); kitty/Shutterstock.com (eye); Shutterstock.com (girl); Tinydevil/Shutterstock.com (butt); Sergieiev/Shutterstock.com (man). 32: Pennyimages/Shutterstock.com (apple); Bernd Schmidt/Shutterstock.com (boy). 33: Alila Medical Media/Shutterstock.com (diagram); Piotr Marcinski/Shutterstock.com (elbow). 34–35: Jorge Felix Costa/Shutterstock.com. 34: Kruglov_Orda/Shutterstock.com (girl); Hung Chung Chih/Shutterstock.com (acrobats). 35: Sebastian Kaulitzki/Shutterstock.com (joints); Inga Marchuk/Shutterstock.com (girl). 36–37: David Lee/Shutterstock.com (bkgrd); Diamond Images/Getty Images (Yankees). 37: Library of Congress, Prints and Photographs Division (Young); Photo Works/Shutterstock.com (Halladay). 38: irin-k/Shutterstock.com (bkgrd); Kostas Koutsaftikis/Shutterstock.com (Pele); Simon Bruty/Sports Illustrated (Hamm). 39: oksana2010/Shutterstock.com (basketball); John W. McDonough/Sports Illustrated (O'Neal). 40–41: Joe Gough/Shutterstock.com (bkgrd); Aspen Photo/Shutterstock.com (girls). 40: Nicholas Piccillo/Shutterstock.com. 41: Library of Congress, Prints and Photographs Division (baggataway); rook76/Shutterstock.com (stamp). 42–43: Stanislaw Tokarski/Shutterstock.com (bkgrd); Tom Reichner/Shutterstock.com (musher). 42: fzd.it/Shutterstock.com. 43: ©Greg Naus/Dreamstime.com. 44–45: Martin Good/Shutterstock.com (bkgrd); Chantal de Bruijne/Shutterstock.com (cyclists). 44: David Stockman/AFP/Getty Images. 45: AFP/Getty Images. 46–48: Shutterstock.com/watchara.

Contents

Chapter 1: Animals
What Is a Dog's Most Powerful Sense?......................................4
What Is the Jacobson's Organ in a Snake? 6
What Is an Aye-Aye?...8
What Are the Differences between African and Asian Elephants?......... 10
What Is a Kookaburra? 12
What Fish Communicates through Farting? 13
What Are Some Fish that Can Walk?.. 14
What Is a Narwhal? 16
What Are Some Mammals that Lay Eggs?................................. 18
What Is the Most Deadly Animal?.. 20
What Is the Oldest Living Animal Species?................................ 22

Chapter 2: The Human Body
What Is the Brain Made Of? 24
What Are Some Ways People Learn? 26
What Is Dyslexia?.. 28
What Is the Strongest Muscle in Your Body?.............................. 30
What Is an Adam's Apple? 32
What Is the Funny Bone? 33
What Does It Mean To Be Double-Jointed?................................ 34

Chapter 3: Sports
What Is a Perfect Game in Baseball?.. 36
What Is the World's Most Popular Sport? 38
What Is an Alley-oop?.. 39
What Is Lacrosse?... 40
What Is the World's Longest Dog Sled Race?............................. 42
What Is the Tour de France? 44

Glossary 46
Index 48

CHAPTER 1 Animals

WHAT Is a Dog's Most Powerful Sense?

You don't have to look far for the answer. It's right under your nose, or rather, a dog's nose! A dog's sense of smell is its primary way of making sense of the world. The lining inside a dog's snout is covered with scent receptors. The amount of receptors varies according to breed. A dachshund has around 125 million, while a beagle has almost twice that amount. People, by comparison, have a mere 5 to 6 million. So it's no wonder that a dog's sense of smell is so much sharper than ours.

Sniffing Around

Dogs sniff in short, rapid bursts of air, drawing scent molecules deep into nasal passageways where they collect in a nasal pocket. The molecules remain in this pocket as the dog continues to inhale and exhale until there are enough molecules for the dog to identify the odor.

A Wet Snout

The tip of a dog's snout, called the leather, is usually moist, and for a good reason. Scent molecules stick to mucous given off by glands inside a dog's nose. As the molecules dissolve, little hairs inside the nose push the scent up the nasal passageways and past the scent receptors.

Get ready to take a walk on the wild side. From man's best friend to egg-laying mammals, the world of animals holds many surprises. In this chapter, you'll meet some fascinating creatures that behave in surprising ways.

Super Smeller: The Bloodhound

The bloodhound has been called a nose with a dog attached, and that's a perfect description for a canine with 300 million scent receptors. A bloodhound's sense of smell is so sharp, its findings are used as evidence in court trials. One Kentucky bloodhound has helped law enforcement agents track down more than 600 lawbreakers.

TRY IT!

How Well Do You Smell?

Humans don't have the smelling ability of dogs, but some people have a sharper sense of smell than others. Gather a group of your friends and take a sniff test.

What To Do

Collect a dozen or so smelly objects from around the house. Here are some suggestions:

- dried oregano or rosemary
- cotton ball soaked with cologne
- mint tea bag
- toothpaste
- vanilla extract
- cinnamon
- mothball
- ripe banana peel
- vinegar
- lemon slice

Have one of your friends sit and close her eyes. Place small amounts of each object under her nose. Ask her to identify the smell. Keep a list of her responses. Take turns until everyone has had a chance, including you. Which person has the best sense of smell? Were some items easier to identify than others?

WHAT'S More...

Researchers have trained some dogs to detect cancer in humans. The dogs can sniff out chemical changes that may signal the disease.

ANIMALS 5

WHAT Is the Jacobson's Organ in a Snake?

When a snake flicks its tongue, the reptile is probably picking up scent particles. A snake relies on its tongue and its Jacobson's organ to identify scents. Located on the roof of a snake's mouth, the Jacobson's organ is a pair of open pits loaded with sensory nerves. After the snake collects airborne chemicals on its forked tongue, it passes the tips over its Jacobson's organ, which turns the chemicals into electric signals. The signals then travel up pathways to the brain. Snakes use their Jacobson's organ to mate and to help them hunt prey.

Thanks to the Jacobson's organ, snakes can hunt by smell alone. One big reason is the forked tongue. Each tip passes over one of the two pits on the roof of its mouth, allowing the chemicals on each tip to be analyzed separately. If a prey's odor is more concentrated on one tip, the snake uses that information to figure out the direction of the animal.

Chemical Messengers

Snakes aren't the only reptiles with a fully developed Jacobson's organ. Lizards, amphibians, and many mammals have this helpful sense organ. The organs are used mostly to detect chemicals called pheromones (*feh*-roh-monz). The chemicals are found in an animal's scent glands, saliva, urine, and feces (poop). They send messages to the brain, such as which animals are ready to mate, that only other members of the same species can understand.

Olfactory bulb (helps the snake process smells)

Jacobson's organ

WHAT'S More...

- The Jacobson's organ was named after Ludwig Levin Jacobson, a Danish doctor and naturalist, who discovered it in 1813.

- People have a Jacobson's organ, but it is not fully developed and doesn't work as a sense organ.

Male lions use pheromones to tell when a lioness is ready to mate. They do this by curling their upper lips into a grimace, which helps to get the scent onto their Jacobson's organ.

Members of the cat family aren't the only ones to curl their lips when they are ready to mate. Horses, buffalo, zebras, and giraffes do too.

Much as a snake uses its tongue, an elephant uses its "finger" at the end of its trunk to gather chemicals and bring them to its Jacobson's organ. This gives the elephant information about other elephants, such as which females are ready to mate and which males to stay away from.

ANIMALS 7

WHAT Is an Aye-Aye?

With big yellow eyes set in a pointy face, large rounded ears, shaggy fur, and an extra-long middle finger that rivals E.T.'s, the aye-aye is one strange-looking creature. But what exactly is it?

Early naturalists believed the aye-aye (*eye-eye*) to be some type of rodent, possibly a squirrel, because its teeth never stopped growing. Modern scientists say the aye-aye is a primate, a close relative of the lemur. The rare and endangered aye-ayes live in the rainforests of Madagascar, an island off the southeastern coast of Africa.

What Long Fingers You Have!

An aye-aye's bony middle finger is long for a reason. It feeds on tiny insects called grubs that live deep inside the wood of trees. To reach these tasty morsels, an aye-aye will first tap on dead wood. When the animal's sensitive ears pick up a hollow sound, it begins to gnaw the wood with its sharp teeth. Then it sticks its middle finger deep inside the hole, using its hooked claw to retrieve its meal.

Aye-ayes are nocturnal, which means they are active at night. In fact, aye-ayes are the largest nocturnal primates in the world. During the day, they sleep in round nests made out of twigs and leaves, which they build in the forks of trees.

Oh, Baby

Females give birth to one offspring at a time. The young aye-aye stays with its mother until it is around two years old, when it leaves to find its own home.

WHAT'S More...

Madagascar, home to the aye-aye, is the fourth largest island in the world. This remote nation in the Indian Ocean is about the size of Texas. Up to 75% of the species that live on the island are endemic, which means they are unique to Madagascar, living nowhere else in the world. The aye-aye is one such species.

AFRICA
Indian Ocean
Madagascar

Happy Feet Lemurs

Another animal found only in Madagascar is the sifaka, a large lemur, a type of primate. Sifakas are most at home in trees, and usually get around by leaping from tree to tree. When they are forced to travel on the ground, they have a unique walk. With arms raised, they hop sideways on their hind legs. No wonder sifakas are also known as "dancing lemurs."

ANIMALS

WHAT Are the Differences Between African and Asian Elephants?

To most people, an elephant is an elephant—a big, grey, wrinkly animal with a long trunk. But there are actually two species of elephant: One lives in Africa and the second in Asia. Here's how you can tell them apart.

Shoulders: Highest part of body

Sloped back

Flat forehead

Large ears that cover its shoulders

Both males and females have tusks.

The front feet have four or five toes each and the hind feet have three.

Two appendages or "fingers" at tip of trunk

African Elephant

The largest land mammal, the African elephant weighs between four and seven tons and stands up to 11 feet tall. There are two subspecies: the savannah (bush) elephant and the forest elephant

Rounded forehead with two humps on the top of its head

Head: Highest part of body

Rounded back

Small ears that don't reach over its shoulders

Females don't have tusks. Only males do.

One appendage or "finger" at tip of trunk

The front feet have five toes each and the hind feet have four.

Asian Elephant

Smaller than its African cousin, the Asian elephant weighs between three and six tons and is around 10 feet tall. There are four subspecies: Indian, Sri Lankan, Sumatran, and Borneo.

WHAT'S More...

Asian elephants were the first species of elephant to be tamed. For thousands of years, people have trained them to plow fields, haul cargo, and carry passengers.

ANIMALS 11

WHAT Is a Kookaburra?

The kookaburra is a bird that lives in the forests of Australia and Papua New Guinea. It is known for its distinctive call which sounds like crazy laughter.

The bird's loud call serves two purposes. It is a way to communicate with other kookaburras and it stakes out territory, letting other birds know that it is not a good idea to move there.

The Bushman's Clock

Kookaburras are early risers, and the forests in which they live fill with their noisy shrieks each morning. They make another ruckus when they roost at night. Because of that, the birds are nicknamed the "bushman's clock." Bushmen, people who live in the forests, can count on the birds to make noises at about the same time each morning and night—like clockwork!

Fierce Hunters

Kookaburras prey mainly on the young of other birds, insects, snakes, and other reptiles. They are fierce hunters, killing their prey by dropping them from the air or bashing them with their bills.

WHAT Fish Communicates through Farting?

Fast Repetitive Tick (FRT) is the name scientists have given to the high-pitched buzzing sound coming out of a herring's anus. Herring, an oily fish found in the waters of the Atlantic and Pacific Oceans, travel in large schools. Scientists think that herring make the sound to communicate at night. Because most fish can't pick up the high frequency, herring can communicate their location to one another without alerting many of their predators. The exceptions are whales and dolphins. These keen-hearing mammals pick up the herring's FRTs and use the signals to hunt the fish.

Breaking Wind Underwater

Scientists believe that herring are the only fish who communicate this way. Some fish make sounds through their swim bladder, a sac located in the abdomen of certain fish. The sac keeps them from sinking. At first, scientists thought that herring used their sac to make sounds. Then researchers noticed that a stream of bubbles from the anal duct appeared at the same time as the noise.

NOISE Pollution

With so many noisy ships' engines in the oceans, noise pollution is a serious problem for many marine mammals. Killer whales that feed almost entirely on herring might not be able to hear the herring's FRTs and won't be able to hunt them as well. And noise pollution might harm the herring's ability to hear and communicate with one another.

ANIMALS 13

WHAT Are Some Fish that Can Walk?

Imagine taking your pet fish for a walk! Impossible you say? A few types of fish, known as walking or ambulatory fish, can travel on land from 20 minutes to as long as several days. Some wriggle their way on land while others use arm-like fins to get around. One fish can even climb trees.

Fishzilla

Some people call the freshwater snakehead fish "fishzilla" because its sharp teeth and long, massive body remind them of a monster. Snakeheads crawl from one pond to another by wriggling their three-foot-long bodies on the ground.

Like the walking catfish, the snakehead is native to China. With no natural predators in the U.S., they can quickly take over a pond or lake, destroying the wildlife.

Catfish

One species of catfish can breathe air and move on land. Walking catfish get around by wriggling, much like snakes do. Native to Southeast Asia, the catfish are now found in Florida. If the fish's home dries up, it will travel on land in search of a new home. The catfish can live on land for several days—as long as their skin stays moist.

Mudskipper

These fish live and skip about the mud in shallow tidal pools. They use their fins like arms to move. When they are out of water, mudskippers breathe through their skin but it must be moist for them to take in oxygen. So they are never far from water.

Climbing Trees

Some mudskippers have suction-like fins on their belly. This makes it possible for them to cling to vertical surfaces, such as trees that grow in their swampy habitats.

WHAT'S More...

Although it's often called the "Mexican walking fish," the axolotl (*ack*-suh-*lah*-tuhl) is not a fish at all. This aquatic salamander belongs to the amphibian family.

ANIMALS 15

WHAT Is a Narwhal?

Found in Arctic waters, the narwhal is a small-toothed whale, a species closely related to the beluga. What makes the narwhal unusual is its teeth. Narwhals have two of them, but in males the larger one pushes through the upper lip and grows into a spiral tusk that can be almost nine feet in length. Female narwhals sometimes grow a tusk, but theirs is much smaller than the male's.

Unicorn of the Sea

The narwhal is most likely the basis for the legend of the unicorn. During medieval times, people believed unicorns really existed. Their proof was the tusks of narwhals that had been brought back from the Arctic by Viking sailors. These "unicorn horns" were believed to have magical properties, such as making poison harmless. Drinking cups made from the ivory tusks were worth their weight in gold.

A Whale of a Baby

Narwhals live together in groups called pods that can contain from two to hundreds of members. The pods can consist of males and females, all males, or all females. An adult male narwhal can grow to be 16 feet long and weigh up to 4,000 pounds. A female gives birth to one baby, or calf, every three years or so. The newborn weighs in at around 200 pounds and is about five feet long.

In Danger

The Inuit, people native to the Arctic, hunt the narwhal for its ivory tusk and its meat. The whale provides an important source of vitamin C in their diet. Hunters, however, are allowed to kill only a certain number of narwhals a year. The real danger to narwhals lies in climate change. The whale lives and hunts near the Arctic coast. As ice melts due to global warming, predators, such as killer whales, can move in and attack. Also, warmer weather makes chunks of ice break off. This creates more icebergs, under which narwhals can get trapped and even suffocate.

WHAT'S More...

- About one in 500 male narwhals sport double tusks.

- The narwhal tusk is the only straight tusk in the world. Tusks of other animals, like the elephant, rhino, and walrus, are curved.

- If chipped, a tusk can sometimes repair itself.

The Narwhal's TUSK

The ivory tusk that sticks out from the whale's head is flexible. It's able to bend about a foot without breaking.

What is the purpose of the tusk? Scientists aren't sure. Some think the tusk helps establish dominance over other males and, like a lion's mane or a peacock's feathers, helps attract females. Some researchers think the tusk might be a sensory organ that helps the narwhal locate food or even figure out sea temperature. But if that's true, why don't most females have tusks?

Male narwhals cross tusks and fight, probably to impress a female.

WHAT Are Some Mammals that Lay Eggs?

When you think of animals that lay eggs, birds, reptiles, and amphibians probably spring to mind, not mammals. Yet echidnas and platypuses, both mammals, do just that. These animals belong to a small group of mammals called monotremes. Like all mammals, monotremes are warm-blooded, have fur, and feed their young with mother's milk. But instead of giving birth to live young, monotremes lay eggs.

Echidna One and Two

There are two species of echidnas and both lay eggs. The short-beaked echidna lives in Australia and Tasmania, an island off Australia's southeast coast, while the long-beaked echidna is found in the highlands of New Guinea. After a female echidna mates, she lays an egg no bigger than a grape directly into a pouch on her abdomen. The egg hatches inside the pouch after a few weeks.

Puggles

Blind, furless, and helpless, the baby echidna, called a puggle, nurses from milk that comes from glands in the mother's skin. The newborn stays in the pouch until it grows spines, about two months later. The puggle still needs to be cared for, so the mother digs her baby a burrow and comes back to feed it until it is ready to live on its own. This happens at around seven months.

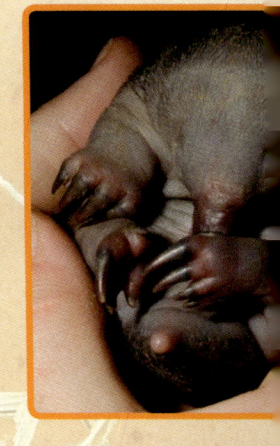

WHAT'S More...

An echidna mother's milk is pink.

What a Platypus

With its duck-like bill, flat tail, waterproof fur, and webbed feet, the platypus is one strange-looking creature. It lives in lakes and streams in Australia and Tasmania. Like echidnas, the platypus lays eggs. However, it does not have a pouch. Instead, the platypus mom-to-be digs a tunnel into the muddy banks and scoops out a "room" that she lines with leaves. She lays one or two eggs in her nest and stays curled over them until they hatch in 10 days. Like echidnas, the platypus doesn't have nipples, so her young lap up milk from patches on her abdomen. The young platypuses remain with their mother for six months before they go off on their own.

WHAT Is the Most Deadly Animal?

You might think a shark, crocodile, or man-eating tiger holds the title of world's deadliest animal. But you'd be wrong. They can't hold a candle to the humble mosquito. Yes, the pest you swat when it buzzes about your head is responsible for an estimated two to three million deaths a year. These members of the fly family spread a number of diseases, including malaria, yellow fever, and West Nile virus.

The Female of the Species

Only female mosquitoes bite. The reason? After a female mates, she needs protein from a blood meal to help her eggs develop. If she isn't developing eggs, she joins male mosquitoes in sipping on flower nectar.

How They Do It

Once a mosquito lands on her prey—that could be you—she pushes her proboscis, a long, slender tube, into the skin. Then, she locates a blood vessel and begins to suck up the blood. The blood goes up one of the two tubes in the proboscis. The other tube is used to inject the mosquito's saliva into the blood vessel. The saliva stops blood from clotting, making it flow more freely and allowing the insect enough time to drink her fill. The reason an itch develops after you've been bitten is because you're having an allergic reaction to the mosquito's saliva.

Injecting Disease

Sometimes a mosquito transmits a disease-carrying organism with its bite. The deadliest of these organisms causes malaria, a disease that kills more than 1 million people each year, mostly in Africa. There is no cure for malaria, but doctors are working on a vaccine to protect people from getting it.

Proboscis

From TIME FOR KIDS

Biting Back Against Malaria

Malaria can be prevented and treated. Unfortunately, many African nations don't have the funds to fight it. Nothing But Nets (NBN), created by the United Nations in 2006, hopes to change that by covering sleeping areas with nets. Hanging bed nets treated with insecticide is a simple yet effective way to stop mosquitoes from biting at night. So far, NBN has delivered more than 7 million nets to countries in Africa. Take that, mosquitoes!

This family in Tanzania will be able to sleep easy under an antimalarial bed net.

Other TOP Killers

- The **box jellyfish** is the world's most venomous, or poisonous, animal. Once stung, a victim has almost no chance of surviving unless treatment begins immediately.

- **Hippos** are super aggressive, territorial, and not the least bit afraid of humans. The combination makes them the most deadly animal in Africa after mosquitoes.

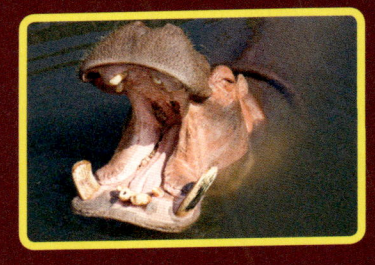

- **White-tailed deer** are gentle forest animals but more than 100 Americans die each year when their vehicles collide with them.

ANIMALS 21

WHAT Is the Oldest Living Animal Species?

The granddaddy of all animal species is the horseshoe crab. A creature that resembles an armored tank, the horseshoe crab has been around for 445 million years or so, more than 200 million years before dinosaurs walked the Earth. Even more amazing, the horseshoe crab looks pretty much the same today as it did back then.

A Living Fossil

Not true crabs but close relatives to spiders, ticks, and mites, horseshoe crabs are called living fossils. If you were to compare an early fossil of the horseshoe crab to one of its living family members, you wouldn't find much difference. It still has the same hinged carapace or shell, the same tail, which it uses to steer itself, and the same compound eyes, each one made up of thousands of lenses.

Living horseshoe crab

Fossil

WHAT'S More...

In the plant world, the ginkgo biloba holds the title of oldest species. The tree has been around for 270 million years.

22 ANIMALS

Immune to Germs

How has the horseshoe crab managed to exist for so many millions of years? Scientists believe it's thanks to the creature's amazing immune system. As soon as bacteria enters the wound of an injured crab, the blood in the surrounding area immediately clots into a gel. This keeps the bacteria from moving forward so the crab won't get sick. This mysterious gel-like substance is called LAL, for short.

Medical Uses

Each year thousands of horseshoe crabs are bled to obtain LAL. The substance is then used in medical labs to test drugs that will be injected into the human bloodstream. The LAL test can quickly and accurately detect if harmful bacteria is present. Horseshoe crabs are doing their bit to keep humans safe.

Some More Living FOSSILS

- The chambered nautilus has lived for the last 400 million years. But today, the mollusk is in danger of dying out. Fishermen hunt the animal for its shell, which is used to make jewelry and decorations.

- Some 350 million years ago, a winged insect, almost exactly like today's cockroach, scurried around on Earth. These almost indestructible insects stand a good chance of being around millions of years into the future.

- The coelacanth (*see*-luh-kanth) is the runner-up in terms of oldest living species. Fossils of this giant fish date back 410 million years.

CHAPTER 2 The Human Body

WHAT Is the Brain Made Of?

Your brain is the commander-in-chief of your body. It tells your heart to beat, your lungs to breathe, and your eyes to blink. The human brain is the most complex human organ. Billions of nerve cells, called neurons, make up the brain. These neurons are connected, constantly interacting with each other as they send messages to all the cells in the body.

If you look at a neuron up close, you can see that it branches off into lots of long spindly ends. One extra-long branch is called the axon. The shorter ones are dendrites. These nerve endings connect to other neurons, passing on and receiving information in the form of electrical signals. The axon sends out signals, while the dendrites receive signals from other neurons.

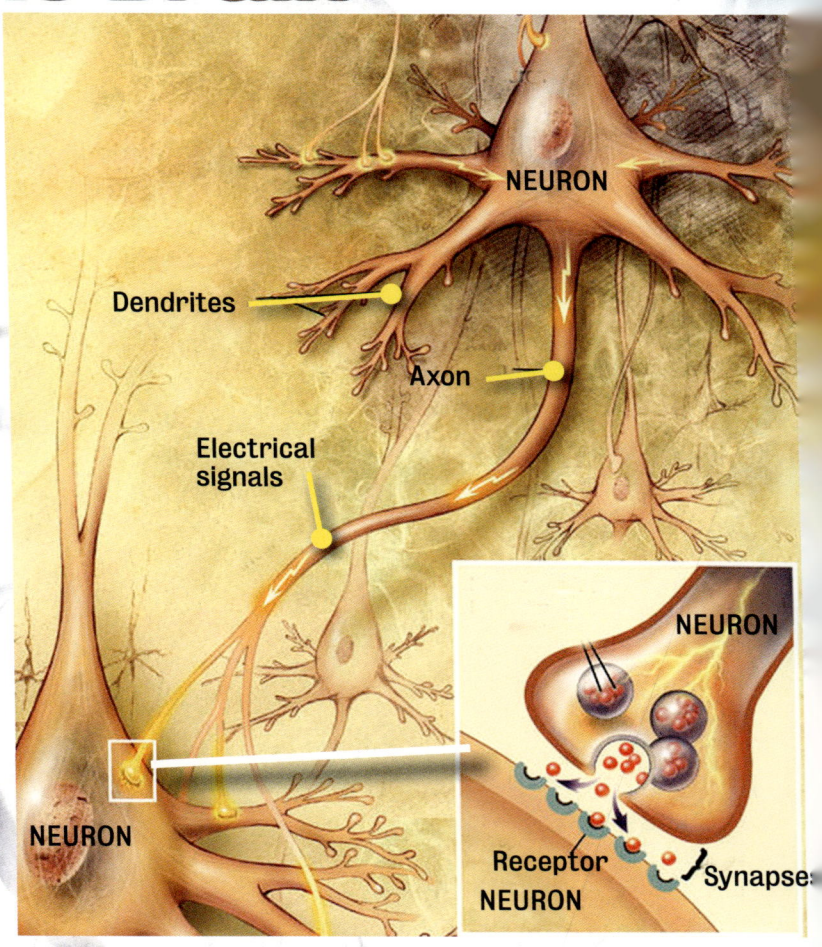

Neurons don't touch one another. Instead they connect by jumping across synapses, tiny gaps between the cells. A synapse releases chemicals that travel across a gap and trigger an electrical impulse in the next neuron.

Is your funny bone really funny—and is it even a bone? What's your gluteus maximus and what's it good for? You'll find out in this chapter as you get to know the ins and outs of your body.

The outer part of the brain, called the cerebral cortex, is grayish in color and has deep folds. This area, where most of our thinking takes place, is extremely dense with dendrites.

The inner area of the brain is paler in color and known as white matter. It's mostly made up of axons. Axons are covered with a fatty substance called myelin sheath, which gives the inner brain its whitish color.

Human Brain Stats

Weight: about 3 pounds

Size: about the size of your two fists put together

Surface area: about four sheets of letter-size paper

Number of neurons: 100 billion

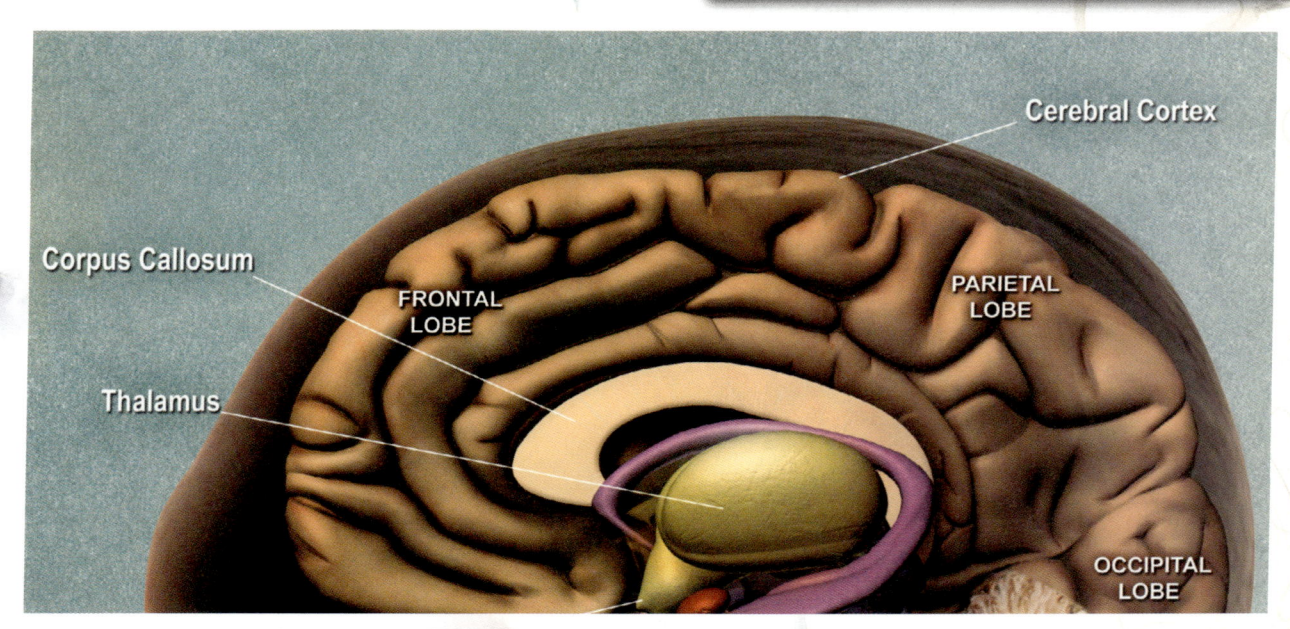

Labels on diagram: Cerebral Cortex, Corpus Callosum, Frontal Lobe, Parietal Lobe, Thalamus, Occipital Lobe

Why are our brains folded? In order to save space and squeeze in as much cortex area as possible. If our brains were smooth, our heads would have to be the size of beach balls!

THE HUMAN BODY

WHAT Are Some Ways People Learn?

There's more than one kind of smart. There are eight! At least according to Dr. Howard Gardner, a Harvard professor who came up with the idea of Multiple Intelligence, or MI. He says that people learn and show their intelligence in various ways. Many scientists now agree with him.

MI is divided into eight different ways of learning. People have ability in all the intelligences, but in different amounts. Take a look at the different kinds of smarts listed below and see if you can figure out how you learn best.

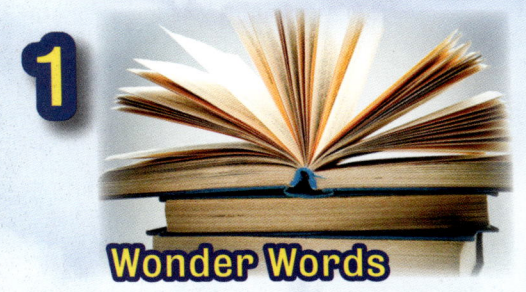

1 Wonder Words
You're good with words. You enjoy reading, writing, and word games. You may find that learning a foreign language will be easy—and fun—for you.

2 Number One Numbers
Calculating math problems comes easily to you. You see patterns everywhere. You probably ace science and math tests.

3 High Notes
You have no trouble picking out a tune's melody or rhythm. You might like to sing, play an instrument, and listen to all kinds of music.

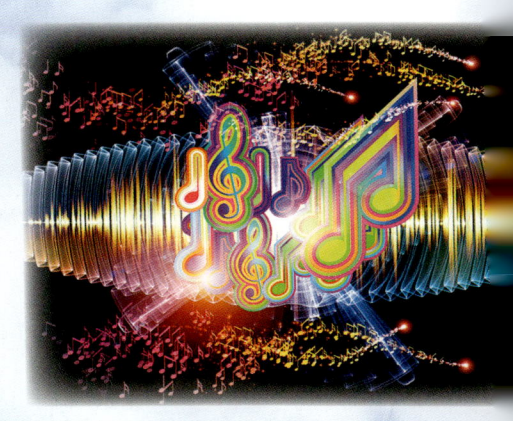

4 Seeing Is Learning
You enjoy looking at interesting objects and possibly have a talent for design. Many artistic people, such as painters, photographers, and architects, have spatial intelligence—they can visualize how things look or work in their mind.

5 Hands On

Are you good at sports? Do you pick up dance steps easily? Or perhaps you're good with your hands and like to make things. People with this kind of intelligence learn by doing.

6 Me, Myself, and I

You're someone who tends to look inward. You know yourself very well, and regularly take stock of your likes and dislikes, your talents, what you're good at doing—and not so good at doing!

7 Getting to Know You

You make friends easily, you're interested in finding out what makes people tick. Psychologists and salespeople have these skills.

8 The Great Outdoors

You love nature. You're interested in knowing the names of plants and animals. You could spend hours gazing at a waterfall or observing a bird build its nest. You may keep a rock collection or be involved in environmental causes.

WHAT Is Dyslexia?

Turn this book upside down and hold it up to a mirror. Now try to read the words. With the letters flipped and reversed, it's very difficult—if not impossible. Many people with dyslexia see words on the page this way. Certain letters might look backwards or upside down. Or the words might appear blurry or seem to jump around.

Dyslexia is a condition that affects a person's ability to read, write, spell, and listen. Someone with dyslexia has a hard time making the connection between the way letters look and the sounds of words. Though learning may be more difficult for kids with dyslexia, it doesn't mean that they aren't smart. It means they have trouble processing what they see, hear, or write into meaningful information.

What Causes Dyslexia?

Scientists believe a glitch in the brain's wiring makes decoding language difficult for some people. Although there is no cure for it, some experts think that if caught early, dyslexia can be reversed. One way to do this is by teaching readers to sound out words, build up vocabulary, and to practice reading. Many dyslexic people discover their own solutions, such as listening to books on tape or asking for extra time to complete tests.

WHAT'S More...

Some kids with dyslexia reverse the order of letters in a word.

As a student looks at a letter, she hears and writes it at the same time. This is one way that kids with dyslexia learn to read.

THE HUMAN BODY

Famous People with Dyslexia

Many successful people have dyslexia. Here are a just a few.

- Bella Thorne, actor
- Keira Knightley, actor
- Meryl Davis, figure skater
- Muhammad Ali, boxer
- Whoopi Goldberg, actor
- Tom Cruise, actor
- Steven Spielberg, director
- Orlando Bloom, actor

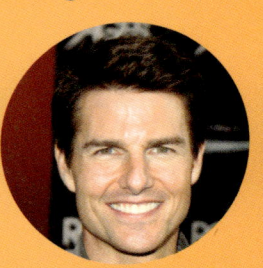

People with dyslexia might experience one or more difficulties reading. Letters that look similar might appear as reversed. For instance, a *b* might look like a *d,* or a *p* like a *q.* Or the letters might appear to swirl about on the page, in constant motion. Words may appear incorrectly spaced, with either too much space between letters and words or not enough, with all the letters squished together.

Thew ord sare n otsp aced cor rect ly.

We spell wrds xatle az tha snd to us.

Sometimesallthelettersarepushedtogether.

WHAT'S More...

Studies indicate that 17% of the U.S. population has dyslexia.

THE HUMAN BODY

WHAT Is the Strongest Muscle in Your Body?

Of the more than 600 muscles in the human body, which one deserves the title of strongest? The answer isn't simple. It all depends on how you define strength. Some muscles have greater endurance or work harder, but when it comes to pure brute force, one muscle rules. Chew on this—it's the jaw muscle. The human jaw can chomp down with a force of up to 200 pounds. It would be the same as having a 200-pound weight coming down on an object. In theory, the jaw is capable of crushing its own teeth.

The Winner: The Jaw Muscle!

THE HUMAN BODY

Here Are Some Other Winners

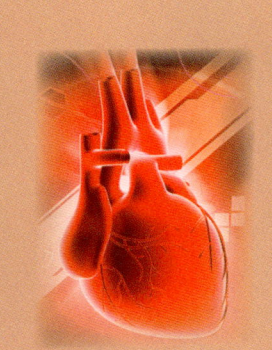

Pump It Up
The heart, which works 24/7, is the body's hardest-working muscle. With each heartbeat, it pumps two ounces of blood and at least 2,500 gallons of blood daily.

Always Moving
Among the smallest muscles in the body, the eye muscles are also some of the strongest. They have great elastic strength and can exert force quickly. When reading, your eyes make more than 10,000 tiny movements per hour.

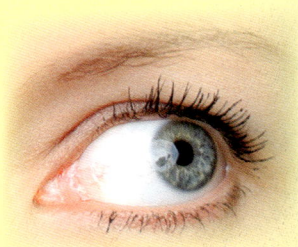

Tongue Twister
Another tough worker is the tongue. Actually a group of muscles, the tongue never quits. It's at work when we eat, speak, and sleep. That's right. At night while we snooze, the tongue pushes saliva into the throat. If you want to see how strong it is, try forcing your tongue down with your finger.

Be Seated
The gluteus maximus—the muscles in the butt—is the body's largest muscle and one of its strongest. It keeps your trunk (the main part of the body from the stomach up to the head) erect.

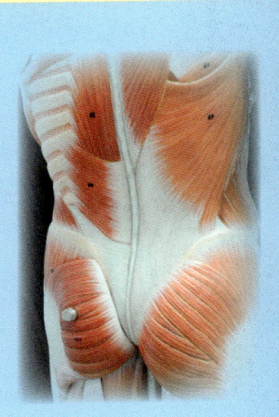

Muscle Men
Bodybuilders work hard at developing their muscles. They pump them up using weight-training exercises that slowly get heavier. They follow a special diet that includes a lot of protein, and they get plenty of rest between workouts. Exercise causes the body's muscles to tear ever so slightly. During recovery, the body repairs these tears, allowing the muscles to grow bigger.

WHAT Is an Adam's Apple?

Ever wonder why your dad's voice is lower and deeper than your mom's? It's mostly thanks to his Adam's apple, that telltale bump on the front of a man's neck. An Adam's apple is made of cartilage, the same flexible substance found in your nose. As a boy gets older, his larynx (*lar*-inks), or voice box, starts to get bigger and the surrounding cartilage grows and hardens with it. In some men, the cartilage sticks out and becomes a bump you can see. That's the Adam's apple.

Why That Name

The Bible tells about the Garden of Eden, and Adam eating the apple that Eve gave him. To many people, the bump in a man's throat looks like a piece of the swallowed fruit.

Name That Tune

Your vocal chords are muscles inside your larynx. The shorter chords produce high sounds, while the longer ones make lower sounds. As boys and girls grow, so do their voice boxes and vocal chords. Boys' grow bigger, so their voices end up lower and deeper.

WHAT'S More...

Because the larynx grows so quickly as a boy matures, his voice sometimes breaks or cracks. After a few months, this stops.

THE HUMAN BODY

WHAT Is the Funny Bone?

Bang! If you've ever hit your elbow in a certain spot, you know that there's nothing funny about the funny bone. In fact, it isn't a bone at all, but a nerve, the ulnar nerve to be exact. The nerve runs from the hand to the shoulder.

Just above the elbow, along the inside of the arm, is a spot where the nerve is exposed. Unlike other nerves, which are protected by muscles or bones, the ulnar nerve is covered only by skin. That's why when we bump or bang this delicate spot, we feel pain.

So why is it called a funny bone? Many people report feeling a weird, tingly feeling when they hit the nerve. Or perhaps it's because the funny bone is next to the arm's humerus (*hoo*-muh-rus) bone, which sounds a lot like the word "humorous."

WHAT'S More...

- The ulnar nerve is the largest exposed nerve in the human body.

- The ulnar nerve controls feeling in your fourth and fifth fingers and in the back of your hand.

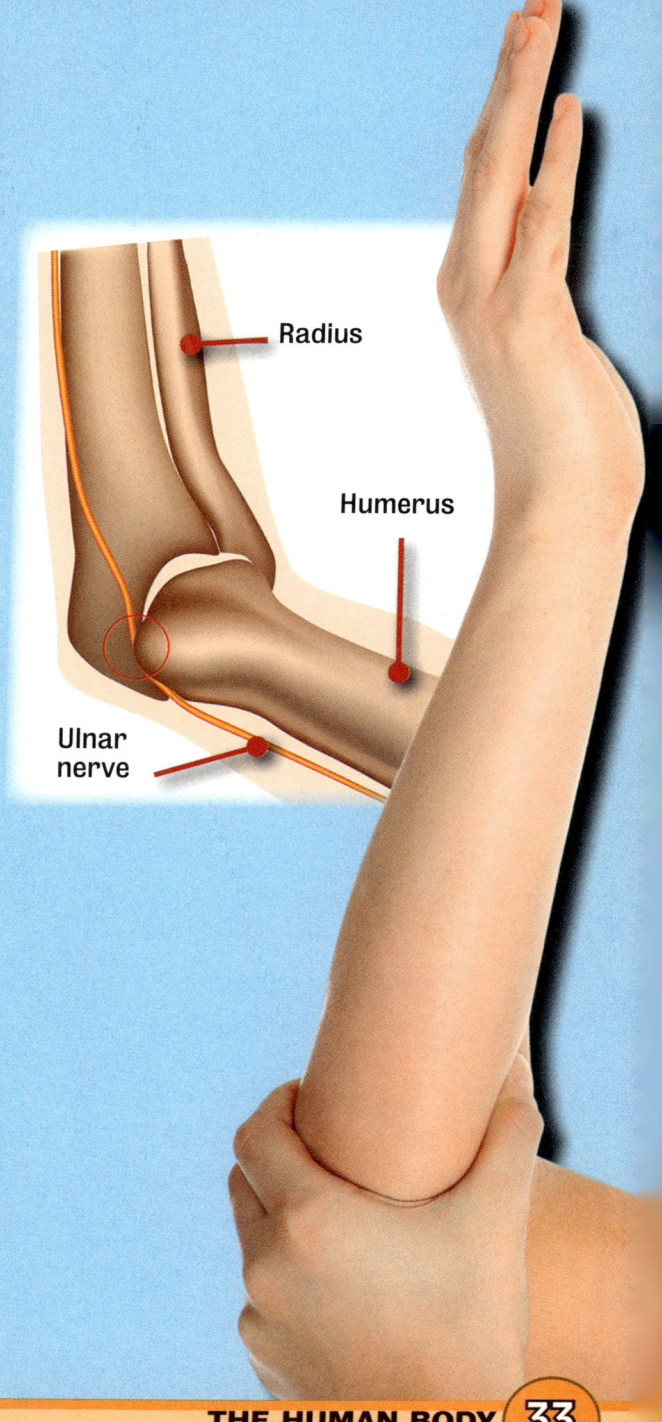

THE HUMAN BODY

WHAT Does It Mean To Be Double-Jointed?

A joint, the place where two bones meet, allows your body to move. Without hip and knee joints, you'd walk around as stiff-legged as Frankenstein's monster or the Tin Man in *The Wizard of Oz*.

So, do double-jointed people have twice as many joints? Not at all. They have the same number as everyone else. It's just that they can bend their joints more than the average person. In some cases, a lot more.

Most joints have a set range of motion. They can only go so far. Some people, though, have a much larger range of motion than others. These contortionists seem to have bones made out of rubber. They can bend and shape their arms and legs into incredible positions.

Circus performers and gymnasts develop great flexibility.

What enables a person to turn into a shape that looks like a pretzel? It helps to know a little about how joints work. Some, like the joints in your knees, swing back and forth, much like the way a hinge allows a door to open and close. Other joints, like those in your neck, pivot and let you turn your head. Ball-and-socket joints work yet another way. The rounded end of a bone (the ball) fits inside the hollowed end (the socket) of another, allowing the bone to move front-to-back and side-to-side. The joints in your shoulders and hips work this way.

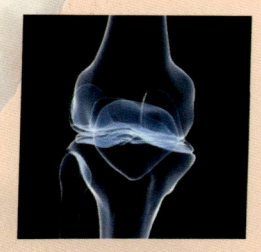

Hinge joint 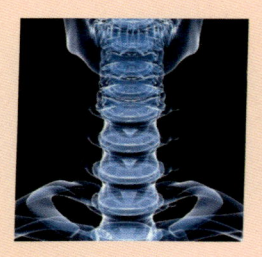   Pivot joint 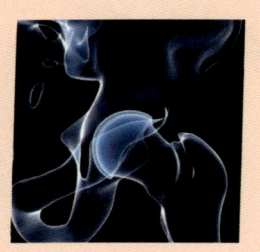   Ball-and-socket joint

What a Joint

People who are double-jointed don't have deep sockets, so the ball part rests shallowly in the socket. This helps joints rotate in any direction. Double-jointed people also have more flexible ligaments (tissue that holds bones together) and tendons (tissue that attaches muscles to bones).

Signs of Being Double-Jointed

- From a standing position, you can touch the floor with the palms of your hands without bending your knees.

- You can bend your fingers all the way back until they almost touch your wrist.

WHAT'S More...

As people age, their bones and ligaments harden. That's why children are more flexible than most adults.

THE HUMAN BODY 35

CHAPTER 3 Sports

WHAT Is a Perfect Game in Baseball?

A perfect game is every pitcher's dream—to face 27 batters and not let any of them get as far as first base. That means no runs, walks, or errors during the entire game which must last a full nine innings. A perfect game is such a rare event that from 1880 to 2014, only 23 pitchers in major league baseball had achieved it.

A pitcher can also shine by throwing a shutout (no runs scored against him) or a no-hitter (no hits against him). In a no-hitter, the pitcher can give up walks and errors. Although it's rare, a pitcher can pitch a no-hitter and his team can still lose. This happened to Ken Johnson of the Houston Colt .45s in 1964. (The team changed its name to the Houston Astros in 1965.) Johnson pitched nine innings against the Cincinnati Reds and didn't allow any hits. His team lost by one run, the result of an error.

WHAT'S More...

The only player to pitch a perfect game in the World Series was Don Larsen in 1956. In Game 5 of the series, Larsen, of the New York Yankees, faced down the Brooklyn Dodgers' 27 batters, striking out seven of them. The Yankees went on to win the series.

New York Yankees catcher Yogi Berra leaps into the arms of Yankee pitcher Don Larsen after winning the 1956 World Series.

Do you know what an alley-oop is? A musher? Would you know what to say? The answers to those questions—and many more—are right here in this chapter. So, start reading. Mush!

Perfect Records

Here are the 23 pitchers who made baseball history by pitching perfect games.

PITCHER	YEAR	WINNING TEAM
Lee Richmond	1880	Worcester
Monte Ward	1880	Providence
Cy Young	1904	Boston
Addie Joss	1908	Cleveland
Charlie Robertson	1922	Chicago
Don Larsen	1956	New York
Jim Bunning	1964	Philadelphia
Sandy Koufax	1965	Los Angeles
Catfish Hunter	1968	Oakland
Len Barker	1981	Cleveland
Mike Witt	1984	California
Tom Browning	1988	Cincinnati
Dennis Martinez	1991	Montreal
Kenny Rogers	1994	Texas
David Wells	1998	New York
David Cone	1999	New York
Randy Johnson	2004	Arizona
Mark Buehrle	2009	Chicago
Dallas Braden	2010	Oakland
Roy Halladay	2010	Philadelphia
Phillip Humber	2012	Chicago
Matt Cain	2012	San Francisco
Felix Hernandez	2012	Seattle

Cy Young

Roy Halladay

SPORTS 37

WHAT Is the World's Most Popular Sport?

You'll get a kick out of this answer! It's soccer—a team sport played in almost every country in the world. More than 3 billion people either play or watch soccer, which is called football everywhere outside the United States. Soccer wasn't very popular in the U.S. until the 1970s. Immigrants to America brought the sport with them and it caught on big time.

Soccer Greats

Voted both Soccer Player of the 20th Century and Athlete of the 20th Century, Pele is the sport's top scorer of all time with more than 1,200 goals. A native of Brazil, Pele retired from soccer in 1977 after playing in a total of 1,363 games.

The U.S. women's Olympic soccer team, led by Mia Hamm, won gold medals in 1996 and 2004. Considered the best female soccer player in the sport's history, Hamm has scored more goals than almost any other female soccer player. Not only that, she's scored 158 goals playing against international teams, the second highest record in the history of the sport. (Pele scored 77 international goals.)

Pele (left) signs a young fan's jersey.

Mia Hamm

WHAT Is an Alley-oop?

An exciting basketball play, the alley-oop requires two players working together to score a basket. Player A looks for an opportunity and passes the ball to Player B, who jumps up, catches it in mid-air, and dunks it into the basket. Like the slam dunk, the alley-oop is impressive to watch. Many half-time shows feature both of these amazing plays to thrill the fans.

One of basketball's most exciting alley-oops helped the Los Angeles Lakers beat the Portland Trail Blazers in a game in 2000. After trailing for the first three quarters, the Lakers were finally winning and wanted to stay in the lead. Kobe Bryant dribbled the ball, jumped, and passed it to Shaquille O'Neal. O'Neal leaped into the air and caught the ball with one hand, and with 40 seconds left on the clock, slammed the ball into the basket. The Lakers won the game, 89-84, and went on to win the NBA championship that year.

WHAT'S More...

Alley-oop comes from the French *allez-oup* (ah-laze-oop), the words a French acrobat says right before making a daring jump or leap. It may have originally meant "to go up."

Shaquille O'Neal gets ready to score a slam dunk against the Trail Blazers.

WHAT Is Lacrosse?

Lacrosse is a centuries-old sport that is a combination of football, basketball, hockey, and soccer. The game is played between two teams on a rectangular field with a goal at each end. Players score by getting a small rubber ball into their team's goal. They do this by scooping, carrying, and throwing the ball with the netted stick. The team with the most goals at the end of the game wins.

In lacrosse, a player's size doesn't matter all that much. Speed and agility do. Players must be fast and have endurance.

Men's lacrosse has 10 players per team, and the games last for four, 15 minute periods. Games can be intense, with a lot of rough body contact which is why men wear protective gear. In women's lacrosse, there are 12 players on each team and the game is half as long. Body contact is not allowed.

In men's lacrosse, protective gear includes a helmet, face guard, and heavy-duty gloves.

Female lacrosse players don't need much protective gear because body contact is not allowed.

North America's Oldest Sport

In the 1630s, European settlers watched Native American tribes play baggataway—a game that uses long sticks and a ball. It was a brutal sport, meant to toughen up its players so they'd become fierce warriors. The field was huge, from 1 to 1.5 miles long. Players numbered anywhere from 100 to 1,000 men. The game could last for days, as players rushed after the ball, flinging it to team members.

Settlers adapted the action-packed sport, called it lacrosse, and started playing it themselves. In 1857, George Beers of Montreal, Quebec, developed rules for the game. In 1882, the first lacrosse league was formed in the United States.

This drawing shows Native Americans playing baggataway, an early form of lacrosse.

WHAT'S More...

The French living in Canada renamed the sport lacrosse after the religious staff used by bishops, called la croix.

SPORTS 41

WHAT Is the World's Longest Dog Sled Race?

Dashing through the snow in a 12-dog open sled… It isn't likely that people who take part in the Iditarod, a grueling sled dog race, would have time to sing that version of *Jingle Bells*. They are too busy driving their dog teams over 1,049 miles of snow and ice in Alaska.

There are two trails, one used in even-numbered years, the other in odd-numbered years. Both start in Anchorage and both end in Nome. On the first Saturday in March, each driver, called a musher, stands at the rear of the sled behind the hitched pairs of dogs. At the signal, more than 50 mushers and their dog teams start the race.

Mushing to the Finish Line

For the next two weeks, humans and animals will face harsh conditions, including below-freezing temperatures, biting wind, and blizzards. Along the way are checkpoints where the mushers sign in so that officials can be sure they are following the correct route and not taking shortcuts.

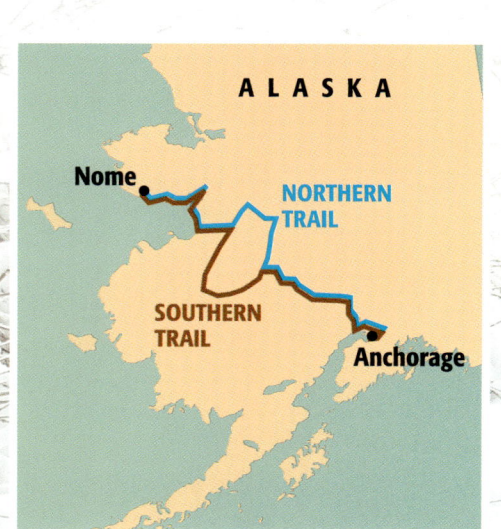

After days of cold and ice and snow, the first musher enters Nome driving the sled toward the finish line, which is a wooden arch. A lantern hanging on the arch stays lit until the last musher glides through as thousands of fans cheer.

Mushers of Tomorrow

The Junior Iditarod is a competition for mushers from 14 to 17 years of age. The 140-mile race gives the teens practice training for the much longer Iditarod. The young mushers and their dogs race for 70 miles, then rest for 10 hours before returning to Anchorage.

The sleds are pulled by teams of dogs. Animal doctors monitor the dogs' health during the race.

WHAT Is the Tour de France?

The Tour de France is a three-week-long, 2,174-mile sprint through France and some neighboring countries. Every July, the best riders from around the world gather to furiously pedal up and down mountains, and sprint along flat surfaces as they head to the finish line in Paris. Along the route, millions of fans cheer the athletes on.

The cyclists ride in teams of nine. Usually only one team member has a chance of winning. The rest are there to help the leader win. How do they do this? By riding in front during parts of the course to shield the leader from wind, by setting a pace for the leader to follow, and by making sure he has plenty of water and other supplies. Team members will even give up their bike to the leader if his breaks down.

The race is divided into stages, each lasting a day. There are 21 stages in all, nine of which take place in the mountains where biking is extra hard. The winner of the Tour de France is the rider with the fastest time overall.

Vincenzo Nibali, winner of the 2014 Tour de France, raises his arms in a victory salute.

About 200 cyclists take part in the Tour de France.

WHAT'S More...

Maurice Garin was the winner of the first Tour de France in 1903. He was disqualified in the 1904 race because of cheating.

Great Moments in Sports

The final moments of the 1989 Tour de France were nail-biting ones. The two leads, American Greg LeMond (left) and Frenchman Laurent Fignon (right), approached the last 15 miles separated by 50 seconds, with Fignon in the lead. In one of the most exciting wins in the sport's history, LeMond whittled down the time second by second. He completed the race eight seconds faster than Fignon, the narrowest tour win ever.

Glossary

amphibian a cold-blooded animal with a backbone, such as a frog, that is born in water and then lives on land when adult

aquatic living or growing in water

Arctic the area around the North Pole

axon the part of a nerve cell that carries impulses away from the body of a cell

bacteria microscopic, single-celled organisms found in water, air, and soil

carapace a hard covering on the back of certain animals, such as turtles

cartilage a tough, flexible type of connective tissue

cells the basic structure of all living things

cerebral cortex the wrinkled outer layer of gray matter in the brain; the part of the brain mainly used in learning

compound eye an eye made up of several simple eyes; most insects have compound eyes

dendrite a nerve cell that carries impulses to the body of a cell

double-jointed having unusually flexible joints that can bend more than most people's

dyslexia a learning disability in which a person has difficulty recognizing and understanding written words

echidna an egg-laying mammal of Australia and surrounding regions that has a long snout and a spiny coat

endangered a species, or type of living thing, that is in immediate danger of becoming extinct, or dying out completely

gland a cell or group of cells that produces a substance that a body uses or gets rid of

global warming an increase in the average temperature of the Earth

grub wormlike larva of certain insects, such as beetles

immigrant a person who moves permanently to another country from his or her native land

immune system cells, proteins, and tissue that protect the body from infection and disease

Jacobson's Organ one of two sacs in the roof of the mouth that certain animals, such as snakes, use to locate smells

joint the part of the body where two bones are connected

kookaburra an Australian bird with a loud, harsh cry

larynx in people, the part of the throat that contains vocal cords

living fossil an animal or plant that closely resembles species known from fossils

Madagascar an island off the southeastern coast of Africa

malaria an infectious disease transmitted by mosquitoes

mammal a warm-blooded vertebrate (having a backbone) that has hair or fur; mammals feed milk to their young.

molecule the smallest part of a substance, made up of one or more atoms

mollusk an invertebrate (animal without a backbone) that usually has a shell that covers its soft body; snails and squid are mollusks

monotreme a type of mammal, such as the platypus, that lays eggs rather than gives birth to live young

musher a person who takes part in cross-country races with a dog team and sled

myelin sheath a fatty wrapping found around certain nerve axons that speeds up neural impulses

narwhal a small whale that lives in the Arctic; the male has a long, twisted tusk

neuron a cell of the nervous system that consists of an axon and dendrites

nocturnal active at night

pheromones chemicals produced by an animal that affect the behavior of other animals

pod a small herd of animals, especially seals or whales

pollution the contamination of air, water, or soil by harmful substances

predator an animal that hunts other animals for food

primate a mammal that has such features as a large brain, five digits on their hands and feet; monkeys, apes, and humans are primates

proboscis a long, flexible trunk or snout of certain animals, such as an elephant's

protein a substance basic to living cells and necessary for an organism to function; it is an important source of energy in a person's diet

species a group of similar organisms

swim bladder an inflated sac found in most bony fish that helps them stay afloat

tendon a tissue connecting muscle to bone

territorial defending one's land or territory

tusk a long, constantly growing front tooth that appears, usually in pairs, in certain animals, such as elephants

ulnar nerve a nerve that runs along the inner side of the arm and passes close to the surface of the skin near the elbow; also known as the funny bone

vaccine a medicine made of dead or weakened germs that prevents a person from getting sick from that germ

venom a poisonous substance produced by certain snakes and insects, usually given off in a bite or sting

Index

A
Adam's apple, 32
Africa, 9, 10
African elephant, 10
Alaska, 42
alley-oop, 39
Arctic, 17
Asia, 10
Asian elephant, 11
Atlantic Ocean, 13
Australia, 12, 18, 19
axolotl, 15
axon, 24
aye-aye, 8-9

B
baggataway, 41
baseball
    perfect games, 36-37
basketball, 39, 40
Beers, George, 41
bodybuilders, 31
brain
    neurons, 24
    parts of, 25
    stats, 25
Brazil, 38
Brooklyn Dodgers, 36
Bryant, Kobe, 39

C
catfish, 14
cerebral cortex, 25
Cincinnati Reds, 36
climate change, 17
cockroach, 23
coelacanth, 23
contortionists, 34-35

D
dendrites, 24
dinosaurs, 22
dog
    bloodhound, 5
    dachsund, 4
    sense of smell, 4-5
    snout, 4
dolphins, 13
dyslexia
    causes, 28
    examples, 28
    famous people with, 29

E
echidnas
    eggs, 18
    puggles, 18
elbow, 33
electric signals
    Jacobson's organ, 6
    in neurons, 24
elephant, 7, 10-11
Evans, Cadel, 44
eye, 31

F
Fignon, Laurent, 45
fish
    herring, 13
    walking, 14-15
football, 40
fossils, 22
France, 44
Frankenstein, 34

G
Garden of Eden, 32
Gardner, Howard, 26
Garin, Maurice, 45
ginkgo biloba, 22
gluteus maximus, 31

H
Halladay, Roy, 37
Hamm, Mia, 38
heart, 31
herring, 13
hippos, 21
hockey, 40
horses, 7
horseshoe crab, 22
Houston Astros, 36
humerus, 33

I
Iditarod, 42
Indian Ocean, 9
Inuit, 17

J
Jacobson, Ludwig Levin, 6
Jacobson's organ, 6-7
jaw muscle, 30
jellyfish, 21
Johnson, Ken, 36
joints
    signs of being double jointed, 35
    types of, 35

K
kookaburrah, 12

L
lacrosse
    protective gear, 40
Larsen, Don, 36, 37
larynx, 32
lemurs, 9
lions, 7
Los Angeles Lakers, 39

M
Madagascar, 9
malaria
    causes, 20
    nets to protect from, 21
    vaccine, 20
mammals, 18-19
math, 26
mosquito
    diseases caused by, 20
mudskipper, 15
Multiple Intelligence, 27
muscles, 30-31
mushers, 42-43
music, 26
myelin sheath, 25

N
narwhal
    in danger, 17
    tusks in, 16-17
Native American tribes, 41
nautilus, 23
neurons
    parts of, 24
New York Yankees, 36
Nigeria, 21
Nothing But Nets (NBN), 21

O
O'Neal, Shaquille, 39

P
Pacific Ocean, 13
Papua New Guinea, 12, 18
Pele, 38
pheromones, 6
platypus, 19
pollution
    noise, 13
Portland Trail Blazers, 39

S
sifaka, 9
smell, 4-5
National Museum of Natural History, 10
snake
    Jacobson's organ, 6
snakehead fish, 14
soccer, 38, 40
swim bladder, 13
synapse, 24

T
Tasmania, 18
The Wizard of Oz, 35
tongue
    in snakes, 6
    in humans, 31
Tour de France, 44-45
tusks
    in elephants, 10-11
    in narwhals, 16-17

U
ulnar nerve, 33
unicorn, 16
United States, 38, 41

V
vocal chords, 32

W-Y-Z
Washington, D.C., 10
West Nile virus, 20
whales, 13, 16
white matter, 25
white-tailed deer, 21
yellow fever, 20
Yogi Berra, 36
Young, Cy, 37
zebras, 7